Woodturning for Beginners Handbook

The Step-by-Step Guide with Tools, Techniques, Tips and Starter Projects

Stephen Fleming

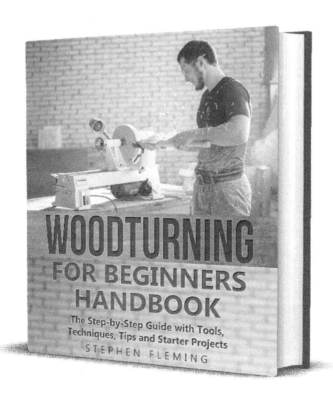

Bonus Booklet

Thanks for purchasing the book. In addition to the content, we are also providing an additional booklet consisting of Monthly planner and Project Schedule template for your first project.

It contains valuable information about woodworking and leathercraft.

Download the booklet by typing the below link.

http://bit.ly/leatherbonus

Cheers!

Table of Contents

Word of caution

Woodturning can turn dangerous as I have seen and heard about many unfortunate accidents while turning; therefore, the utmost priority should be given to safety and security while practicing this activity.

I will share all my experience in this book, but it is essential to remember that, just like various other kinds of woodworking, woodturning is naturally risky.

Failure to use devices and tools appropriately or not adhering to recommended safety standards could result in significant injury or death.

It's your responsibility to make sure you understand your tools and devices and how to use them properly before attempting a woodturning task.

Make sure to read, recognize, and adhere to the most current guidelines and safety precautions for your lathe and various other devices.

Any book, video, or any other means of learning can't replace learning physically from an expert. These forms of information are only additional guidance to be used along with a practical demonstration and training from an experienced woodturner.

All the projects mentioned are my way of doing it. The same projects can be executed differently by other woodturners. So use any technique at your own risk.

So to sum it up: The first and foremost tip is to wear all the safety equipment and follow safety guidelines every time you practice woodturning.

PREFACE

"If you don't blow up a bowl now and then, you are not aren't trying hard enough"- D. Raffin, Master Woodturner

When I first started woodcraft, I looked desperately for a go-to guide about the processes and tools I would need.

The content I found online was total information overload and wasn't presented sequentially. The books I looked at were either focused on just a few processes or assumed that I already had the necessary information. A lot of the books were also very dated.

There are two ways of learning; one is learning from SMEs (Subject Matter Experts) with years of experience, and the other is to learn from people who are just a few steps ahead of you in their journey.

I fall into the latter group. I have spent five years on this hobby and am still learning from the experts.

I still remember the initial doubts I had and the tips that helped me.

This book is for those who are still running their first lap (0-3 years) in wood-crafting and want to have a holistic idea of the processes and tools they need.

I have included photographs of realistic beginner projects, and I will explain the processes and standard operating procedures associated with them.

In the last chapter, I have provided tips for beginners and a glossary of woodturning terms.

Cheers, and let's start the journey.

Stephen Fleming

1. Introduction to Woodturning

What is Woodturning

Woodturning is the art and craft of developing designed wood items on a lathe.

The lathe is a device initially created over 3,000 years ago, that holds and rotates a material like timber or rock to ensure that it can be rapidly carved with sharp tools.

Woodturned items vary from the baseball bat, chair ad table legs to rolling pins, ceremonial bowls, and also modern-day sculpture.

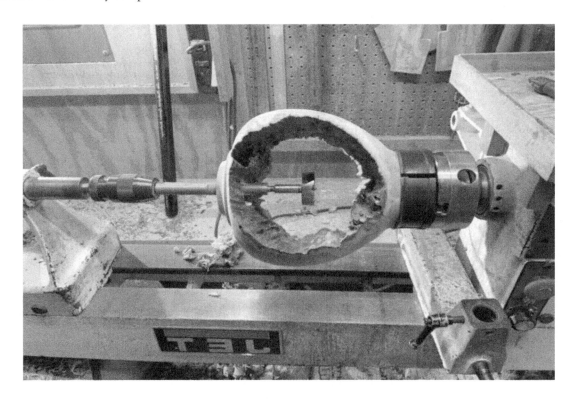

Woodturning is an enjoyable art - the procedure moves quickly, and shavings fly as the woodturner works. Turning is an exciting process at many levels: it is a pleasant task to learn, and with a little bit of effort, the beginner can soon end up with some excellent things.

Becoming a woodturner needs a method as well as a deep understanding of the properties of various types of timbers, the constant improvement of a technique, knowledge of surfaces, as well as a solid determination to learn the basics and make something you like.

Lathes range tremendously in dimension, from a small watch manufacturer's handheld lathe to lathes over a hundred feet long for making masts. Lathes can be powered by a motor, water, or a human, but they all execute the very same task: spinning timber so that it can be sculpted. From a single machine in the hands of the competent turner, comes a vast and remarkable selection of items.

As we know now, woodturning is shaping the wood while it rotates. The timber can be spinning at a very fast rate, so there are threats involved. It's a great idea to think about safety and security first.

Introduction to Woodturning Terminologies

1. Personal Protective Equipment (PPE)

I understand that PPE (Personal Protection Equipment) can sound boring, but it is essential. Additionally, it's not that boring, and the coolest woodturners must have the best PPE.

Eye protection: I wear a visor that offers a good deal of security from prospective accidents. A visor is likewise a fantastic option if you are like me and wear glasses.

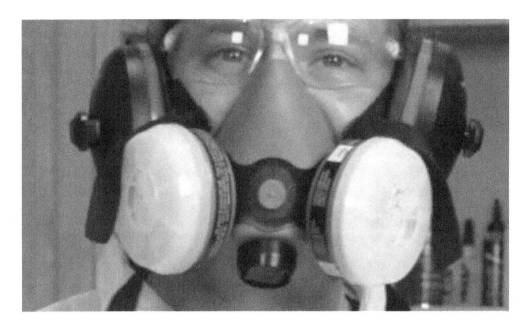

The second-best choice for keeping your eyes safe and risk-free are safety glasses. These are ideal for clarity of vision. I prefer to keep an extra pair for an emergency.

Foot protection: This isn't discussed much, but things could end up badly if you dropped something sharp on your foot.

Durable footwear will shield your feet from falling tools.

Boots or similar shoes with a steel toecap will do a much better job keeping all your toes safe.

Lung protection: This is often a somewhat overlooked aspect, but very important. Wood dust can cause asthma, which carpenters and joiners are four times more likely to get compared with other similar workers.

You can opt for a respirator with good quality filters. A proper respirator will not be uncomfortable to use and will keep your airways functioning well.

You can also get a dust extraction system. They are noisy but useful tools. The best thing about the system is that you can hook them to different shop machines, and this will remove wood dust from the area.

2. Lathe Security

I have mentioned this already, but it's essential to make sure you understand:

Woodturning can be hazardous; unlike most tools in a workshop where things cutting the timber move a little bit, the wood is rotating very quickly, so you need to think seriously about security.

We can minimize the threats, but they are still most likely to exist in some form or other, so always be careful around power devices and try to think ahead about what you are about to do and also what might go wrong.

- **Speed**

I would always advise you to start turning at a slower rate and gradually speed your lathe up until it is going fast enough to function properly. If you turn something that is not correctly balanced, it is most likely to trigger your lathe and the timber to vibrate. The more significant and more out of equilibrium, the more noticeable this issue will be, and the more likely it is that the timber will break and be flung far from the lathe. You'll be glad you are wearing a visor/screen if it hits your face. Better to damage the visor than your flesh.

If you have something huge and out of balance, you can start at a slow rate and create a balance gradually by shaving timber off one side. This will make the work a lot better balanced before you boost the speed.

3. The Tool Set

Woodturning requires a few tools, along with a lathe. I would suggest a newbie get a basic set at first, and discover just how to utilize them before adding to your collection.

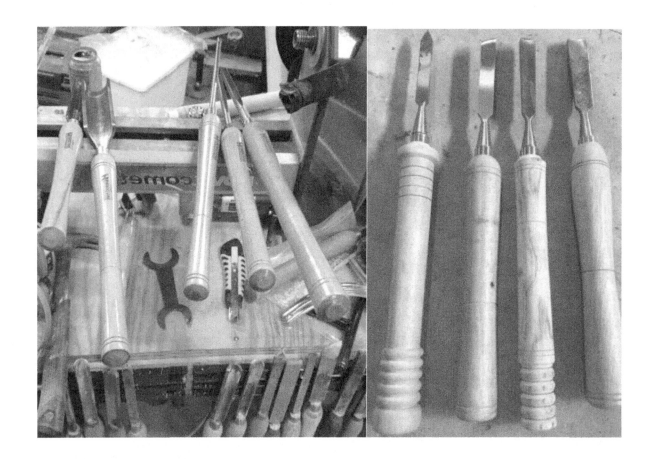

There are a great number of different turning devices out there as well as a lot of different grinds or adjustments you can do to impact the performance of your tools. Don't worry if you don't have them all to start with.

4. The Lathe

See the picture of the lathe with different parts.

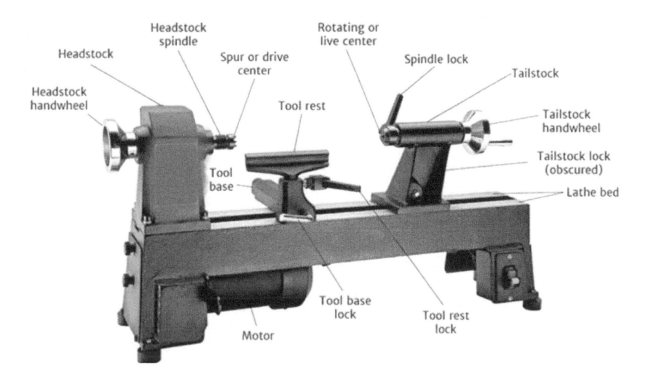

The large one: This is the one that transforms the timber. All the parts of this tool are necessary. Yet possibly the most crucial is the on-off button.

Head supply: This is the part where all the power originates.

Drive center: There are different kinds that aid in holding a job when pin turning (Pin job is transforming between centers- (the head and tailstocks).

Tailstock: The tailstock holds an online facility -comparable to a driving facility yet allows it to rotate.

Banjo and tool rest: The banjo holds the tool rest for permitting it to be transferred to the ideal position.

Turning: The device remainder allows acquisition for your turning tools to work. You rest the cutting tool on this when turning. Without the tool remainder, your devices would knock into the lathe bed and have a high probability of harming on your own or damaging your workshop.

Lathe bed: the bottom part of the lathe is the tailstock, and also banjo can slide up and down and be locked into the area as required.

5. Chuck

A chuck is a specialized sort of clamp made to hold an item with radial proportions, particularly a cylindrical tube. In drills as well as mills, it holds the revolving tool, whereas, in lathes, it holds the revolving workpiece. On a lathe, the chuck is installed on the spindle, which revolves within the headstock.

6. Spindle Roughing Gouge

It is a large tool transferring most of the weight.

It makes a rough shape but leaves a reasonable finish.

If you want to turn a square blank and make it round, the spindle roughing gouge is the best tool to use.

Avoid using this tool to make a bowl as there is a risk of breaking down due to its weak point going into the handle.

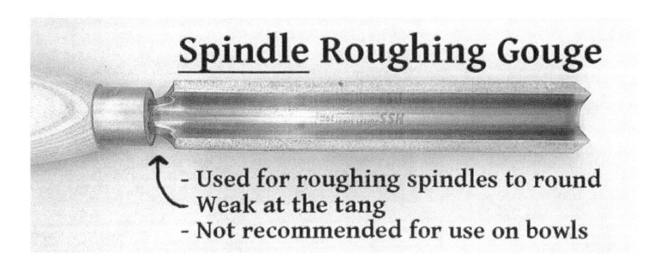

Spindle Roughing Gouge

- Used for roughing spindles to round
- Weak at the tang
- Not recommended for use on bowls

Roughing out

This is the best tool for roughing out the surface, so it is aptly named.

Always follow the golden rule: cut from high points to low points.

Also, use a stance where you can move easily, allowing your body to run the tool.

7. Spindle Gouge

This tool is used to make beads, curves, and can be made use to form spindle work without much hassle.

Spindle gouge

If you have used the roughing gouge, this is used similar but is a much smaller size. Beveling the spindle gouge before use still applies.

With this tool, you may wish to think about placing in some other shapes like beads as well as curves.

8. Skew Chisel

Mainly used as a device for planing the wood, it transforms the wood surface, making it very smooth, so it needs practically no sanding.

It can be used to develop detailing, and it can be utilized for many other tasks.

This device has a reputation for being tough and challenging to handle. But as soon as you understand how to use it properly, it will be a beneficial tool.

If you focus your complete attention on this tool, it will only take a little while to get used to it. I, too, had my share of accidents with this tool, and now I understand that the skew chisel demands total focus.

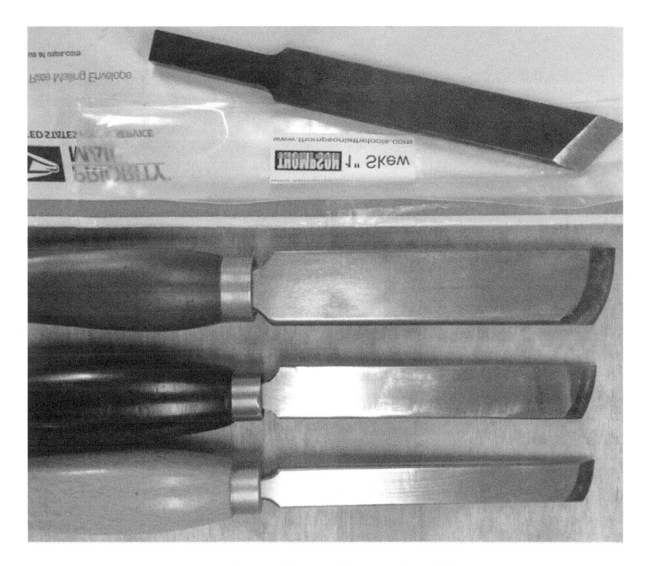

When using, it is imperative to make use of the middle part of the blade. If you strike the revolving timber with the end parts, they are likely to catch and ruin your work. This isn't the end of the world. However, it can be a little scary if you're not expecting it.

The skew chisel can be used to do a variety of things; however, it tends to be recognized for its capacity to offer planing cuts. I like to adjust my tool rest to make the wood as level as possible.

9. Parting Tool:

One of the fundamental tools in the woodturning collection is the parting tool.
 It is manufactured in lots of sizes, yet if asked by newbie, I would advise the 6mm (1/4in) identical parting tool.

The basic operation of this tool is to part or divide the timber into two separate pieces; however, it is made use of primarily to make sizing cuts, such as fillets on pin turning or spigots for chucking techniques. The parting device has lots of uses and also is an important part of any type of woodturning basic tool kit. As with any kind of device, it will only cut efficiently when it is sharp.

The parting tool is without question the simplest tool to develop as the side is short; however, the bevel is long. When sharpening the parting tool, it needs to be ground square at the end rather than at a skewed angle.

10. Bowl Gouge

As the name suggests, bowl gouge is a hand tool used to cut and form timber bowls on a lathe. The bowl gouge includes a handle linked to a sturdy steel shaft.

Bowl Gouge
- Used for turning bowls
- Strong, solid round bar
- Can also be used on spindles

Bowl Gouge   Spindle Gouge

11. Swept Back Grind Bowl Gouge

This is virtually like a regular bowl gouge yet the end is different

A bowl gouge has a straight work; a swept-back grind is even more of a U shape that enables the wings of the tool to be used as cutting edges.

This makes the device very flexible, enabling a better range of cuts.

This bowl gouge provides you with more options, mostly due to the wings.

While making a dish with the swept-back bowl gouge, you can utilize the wings for cutting and then dragging back to the edge of the bowl.

If you do not rub the bevel, you could risk a catch, or the tool may cut a lot more aggressively than you were initially anticipating.

12. Scraper

Scraper- these come in various profiles and act in a comparable way to a cabinet scraper.

Some turners truly love them while others do not.

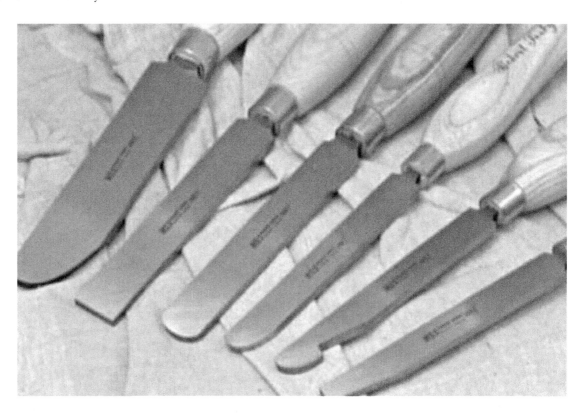

The major disadvantage of using a scraper is preparing the device with a cutting burr.

I have watched timber turning video clips where the turner used only a scraper. The device is really for finessing instead of doing the heavy training.

13. Sharpening Your Tools

I think the one thing that truly pays off when turning is making sure you have sharp tools.

Sharp tools make woodworking enjoyable as it takes away the unnecessary work and gives you much better results.

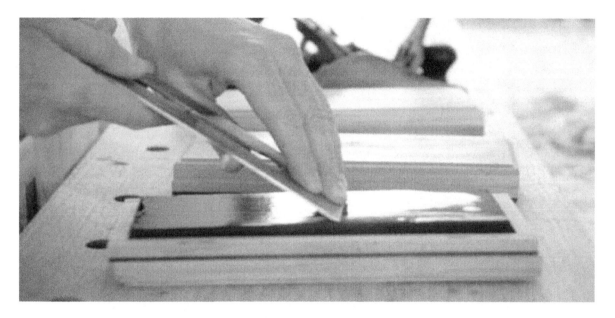

There are many sharpening systems around with associated jigs to guarantee you can reproduce specific grinds.

I would recommend discovering exactly how to utilize your sharpening system for your tools- each method will be a little different.

14. Types of Turning

There are two main types of turning. Spindle Turning and Face Work.

The techniques utilized are somewhat interchangeable; however, there are distinctions to remember.

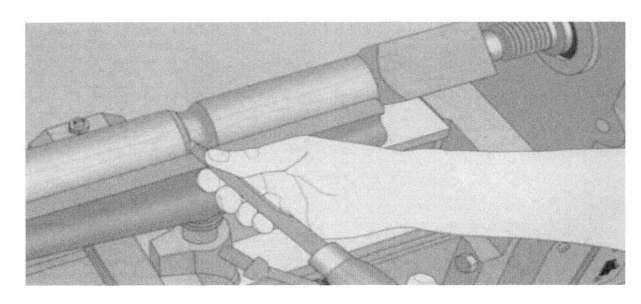

Spindle Turning

If the grain of the wood remains in line with the spindle or bed of the lathe, it is called Spindle Turning. It does not matter if you are making a chair leg or a flower holder; this is still Spindle turning.

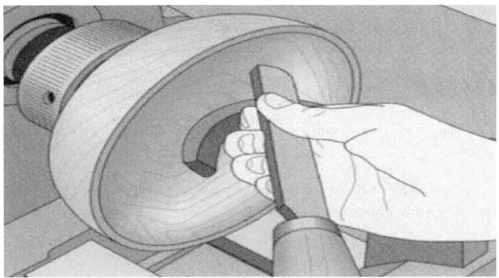

Face Work

If the grain of the timber is at right angles to the lathe axis, then this is called Face Work. A lot of bow turning is a face job.

These definitions are necessary since they establish which tools will be used for a project.

Sanding

It is much easier to do the sanding as part of the woodturning process. This step is messy, so ideally put on a dust mask and also use a dust extractor.

The dos

Develop the grit. The lower the number on an item of sandpaper, the more aggressive it is. Depending on your skills with the tools, you may intend to use coarse paper to hide mistakes, yet even if you don't, you might have some changes that could need a little easing.

The grit dimension of sandpaper is the number, which is inversely related to the fragment dimension. A small number such as 20 or 40 indicates a coarse grit, while 1500 shows a fine grit.

Modification Directions: You could be tempted to allow the lathe to do all the jobs; however, this might not offer the most effective results. The grit of the sandpaper may make red stripes; to stop this from happening, stop the lathe after you finish each grit. This will separate all the unwanted lines.

Finishing

The important thing is to think about how your object is going to be utilized. If it's likely to be used and washed a whole lot, you might want to think about a melamine/ plastic or even CA surface finish.

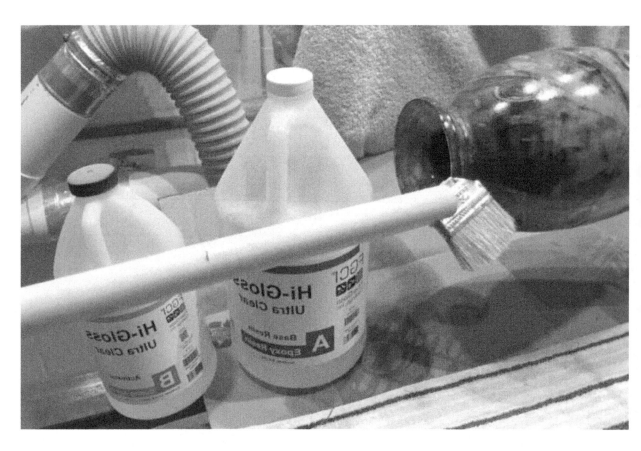

If it will be used with food or is a plaything, you will need to find a safe or food-safe coating. If you desire a finish that is easy to apply, you could use an oil coating like Danish oil or perhaps wax.

You might additionally want to think about coloring the project.

Generally, there are three groups of wood toxicity: irritability, sensitization, and poisoning.

Inflammation/Irritation

Skin, breathing tracts, and mucous membranes are often aggravated by any fine dirt or sawdust because it takes in moisture, consequently drying out the surface area with which the dirt is in contact.

Itchy skin, and sneezing, are two examples of fundamental inflammation of fine sawdust. The degree of irritation is equal to the exposure time and the concentration of wood dust.

However, irritability is not always benign. Woods like walnut and rosewood emit pleasant odors with low levels of dirt, which most woodworkers associate with being just one of the advantages of dealing with timbers. Nevertheless, the natural compounds in these woods that cause the aromas are also possibly toxic with higher dosage and direct exposure.

The long-term results of exposure to wood dust can include allergies to the dust or, potentially, nasal cancer.

Sensitization

Materials in timber that trigger a rising allergy after frequent exposure is called sensitizers.

This kind of toxicity is specific to people and takes time to establish - some individuals may experience a considerable reaction to the wood while others do not.

While sensitization generally requires time and repeated direct exposure to create, it is feasible for some people to have an allergic reaction to a timber upon their first exposure to it.

Even if you do not respond to a timber (or its dust) the first couple of times you are exposed to it, it's still vital that you take precautions and stay clear of as much direct exposure as possible. Your body is more likely to establish a reaction the more you are exposed.

Poisoning

Widely dangerous chemicals are hardly ever discovered in all-natural timber that's available on the business market.

Most poisons in plants and trees are located in the bark and/or sap-- there are some exceptions for rare woods.

In some cases, harmful chemicals are present in timber items, such as when the wood is pressure-treated wood for kitchen cabinetry, flooring, or furniture.

Some more common timber demands that woodworkers understand their own allergies. Those that have an allergic reaction to aspirin must avoid using timbers from birch and willow trees (Betula spp. and Salix spp.) because these have a good amount of salicylic acid, the essential active ingredient in aspirin.

Prevention

You can limit your exposure to wood dust by complying with the following points.

Safety Gear   Dust Collector

1. Usage a vacuum cleaner for dirt collection in your workshop, as well as making sure your shed is aerated with fresh air.

Dust Collector

2. Use safety devices while woodworking: dust mask, goggles or a full-face respirator, and also a protective barrier such as lotion. Apply lotion to arms or exposed skin.

3. As soon as you have finished woodworking, change your garments, wash them, and take a shower. This will certainly prevent wood dust from being transferred to your home, where you or your household would be repeatedly subjected to it.

What about the toxicity of wood in my finished project?

"Not to omit any one of them, the yew is similar to these other trees in general appearance. It is an ascertained fact that travelers' vessels, made in Gaul of this wood, to hold wine, have caused the death of those who used them."

–Pliny the Elder, from *Naturalis Historia,* ca. 77 AD

Infant baby cribs and also food utensils are frequently projected that woodworkers are interested in, and that needs to be made from 'safe' woods and finishes. In short: a sealed and finished wood poses no risk of poison.

What sealant or finish should you use? Solvent-based finishing items (lacquer, varnish, etc.) are highly hazardous in their fluid state, yet when used and dried, both finishes are completely safe.

For projects such as salad bowls and cutting boards that will be in contact with food, you truly don't desire a hard shell finish (lacquer or varnish) that can chip or rub off. Mineral oil, teak oil, and butcher block oil are all common and secure selections for these projects.

**Link to the full list of wood allergies and toxicity https://www.wood-database.com/wood-articles/wood-allergies-and-toxicity

WOOD SPECIES	REACTION	AREA(S) AFFECTED	POTENCY
Abura	irritant, nausea, giddiness, and vomiting	👁	★★☆☆
African Blackwood	irritant, sensitizer	✋👁🫁	★★★☆
Afrormosia	irritant, nervous system effects, asthma, splinters go septic	✋👁🫁	★★★☆
Afzelia	irritant, sneezing	✋👁🫁	★★☆☆
Agba (Gossweilerodendron balsamiferum)	irritant	✋	????
Aglaia (Aglaia genus)	irritant	✋🫁	★★☆☆
Ailanthus	irritant	✋	★☆☆☆
Albizia	irritant, nausea, pink eye, giddiness, nose bleeds	✋👁🫁	★★★☆
Alder (Alnus genus)	irritant	✋👁🫁	★☆☆☆
Alligator Juniper	irritant	✋🫁	★★★☆
Amboyna	irritant, asthma	✋🫁	????
Andiroba	irritant, sneezing	✋👁🫁	★★☆☆

Reference: wood-database.com

2. Process & Techniques

Wood Turning Types

Green Turning: Turning freshly cut timber that has a high moisture content is called Green Turning.

It is simple, as devices quickly cut the timber and create less dust.

Nonetheless, since wood contracts as it dries out, a green turning may warp or fracture.

Some turners deliberately allow the timber to misshape so that each completed piece has a unique form. Others try to lessen the distortions by turning a piece twice.

The first turning is done when green, leaving optimum thickness so that it dries out well. The second round happens after it is dry, and gives the final shape.

All-natural edge turning: An item that includes the outer tree trunk or limb as its side.

Imaginative turnings and natural-edge things made using this technique are typically bowls or hollow vessels.

Multiaxis Turning: The method of turning a solitary piece numerous times, utilizing various sets of centers each time. You can remount the job item by hand or utilize a unique chuck that can be used to hold the workpiece off its exact center.

Ornamental Turning: This is an approach that calls for a specialized machine called a rose engine lathe. The piece is placed on a rocking headstock, and a spinning tool cuts unique and ornamental patterns.

Segmented Turning: Any turning that includes numerous tiny items of wood in its layout. Segmented turnings consist of ones where the entire turning is made from sections and those where just a small portion of the turning is fractional. Larger segmented turnings can consist of several thousand pieces of wood, all precisely cut and assembled to form unique layouts or pictures.

What do you require to start woodturning?

You require something that will rotate timber. A tiny beginner's lathe is an excellent option; you don't need a huge, strong lathe to start with. One more choice is to make your very own lathe using a drill or a drill press if you're feeling creative.

What's the distinction between a huge and a small lathe?

Mini Lathe   Large Lathe

Generally, the size of the wood to be turned decides which type of lathe to use.

If you wish to turn bigger pieces, then a larger lathe is needed. For example, smaller sized desk lathes can turn about 10 inches in size, whereas bigger lathes can turn up to 24-inch bowls.

The bed length is an additional distinction. Bigger lathes have longer bed lengths; however, many smaller lathes also come with an extension.

A bigger lathe will certainly be sturdier and can also deal with extra-large items of wood without shaking. Nonetheless, if you secure your lathe appropriately and use moderately sized items of wood, you won't have much of a concern, regardless of what size lathe you have.

What accessories do you require?

Most lathes come with a faceplate, a spur center, and a live center for the end, and that's all you need to get started other than the turning tools.

Do you require a chuck?

Chuck

Well, it depends. Many individuals turn with chucks, but a lot of individuals become proficient woodturners without one. Certain items are less complicated to turn using a chuck, such as hollowed-out boxes and bowls; however, there are many other items you can turn that you don't need a chuck for.

What kind of devices do you require?

So you have the ideal tools and modern-day carbide cutting tools. The primary difference between both is the learning curve. Carbide cutting devices are simpler to utilize at once, whereas with typical tools, it takes a bit longer to learn the right method.

Additionally, you need to hone the conventional devices with a grinder as you use them, to keep them sharp; nevertheless, that's not a problem with the carbide cutting ones, as you can change the tips when they become dull.

The two types are utilized differently. A conventional tool like a roughing gouge, for example, is held at an angle, pointing up in the direction of the timber as you're cutting, whereas the carbide devices are held directly.

What are the actions of establishing the lathe?

When you have unboxed your lathe, first of all, place in your spur center and your real-time center, and make sure they are satisfactorily in the middle on center; that is important if you do spindle turning.

One more beneficial thing is putting down some WD40 or various other lube on the bed to make everything slide more smoothly. Make sure you re-apply the lubricant every time you turn.

If you have a desk lathe, it must be screwed down to secure it.

Likewise, be sure to examine your belts, so they're on the appropriate rate of what you're attempting to do.

When do you use various speeds?

When initially establishing an item of timber on the lathe, begin slowly.

If the lathe starts to wobble, decrease the speed. Then as soon as your piece is centered, you can increase the speed.

Be aware that if you're working with an item of timber with issues in it, you intend to be much more cautious and begin the rate out slower; otherwise, it can break down.

Can you turn any kind of wood?

Fundamentally, you can turn with any timber; however, it's a great idea to steer clear of anything treated and compressed. Additionally, certain tropical woods like cocobolo and rosewood can cause some irritation. It doesn't trouble all individuals, yet some people have a worse reaction to those than others.

Also, no matter what kind of timber you're turning, it can trigger issues if you inhale the dust. Remember to wear a mask or a respirator.

Turning different timbers

While you can turn any timber, certain woods are softer to turn, and others are harder. As an example, mounting lumber is soft, whereas hardwoods like walnut and maple are harder. After that, specific timbers like applewood or cherry are also more challenging to turn than walnut but are also more beautiful when turned.

When do you turn damp vs. completely dry wood?

You utilize dry timber when you don't intend to have movement anymore after it's turned. If you're making boxes, you might use completely dry timber; by doing this, your lid does not go out of shape.

Greenwood (or wet timber) is frequently used for bowls. Initially, you rough turn when the timber is wet, then allow the dish to dry completely for about a year, and after that turn it finely once again.

Damp timber is also very different to turn than dry wood. It's much softer as well as much more comfortable to turn and a great deal more enjoyable!

Why get a lathe?

Well, woodturning opens up many doors as well as enabling you to do things that are hard to accomplish by other means. It's a great way to digitally detox and an exciting way to pass the time.

As an example, if you're making a table, you can turn round legs with various designs on them for it. Bowls and plates can be made on the lathe, in addition to spindles, baseball bats, knobs, and various other things that belong in the "round family" of items.

How to Pick a Timber for Turning

There are four major factors you can use to narrow the field when choosing timber for turning:
1. Rate/Price
2. Shade/Color
3. Durability
4. Workability

Rate/Price

This might seem obvious, yet it is a reasonable place to start.

Regardless of your woodworking understanding, you will know how much you can invest in the job; this can remove a lot of expensive alternatives that you don't need to consider.

Now, you might be thinking, " However, I have no idea what price various timbers are?".

That's fine, while I promote buying from your local timber stores when possible, you can make use of online stores as a pricing source even if you don't buy from them (and in some cases, you need to buy online since your local vendor may not have what you require).

Most likely a site like WoodWorkersSource.com or. BellForestProducts.com will have many choices, and you can also look for what size blank you need within a given price range.

This will certainly offer you a concept of what timbers you should be looking into.

When you have a checklist of hardwoods in your rate range, you can begin to choose further.

Shade/color

I'll proceed and address before you ask: yes, you can stain an item of light timber. However, this will certainly not provide you with the same look as the original colored wood, and if your piece ever gets damaged, it will show up light, but it can be a means to obtain a beautiful looking item at a lower price to start with.

Regarding shade, it will undoubtedly be only approximately what you desire for your task.

This is merely an additional qualifier than can help thin out a substantial sea of great options.

If you wish to make an item of wood darker, several choices can be more suitable than staining. I'll offer you three examples:

1. Ammonia fuming: a procedure whereby wood is exposed in a contained setting to the fumes that ammonia emits as it vaporizes over a fairly brief time period. The timber will come to be considerably darker or even virtually black.

2. Burning: A darkening process where a torch scorches timber, then the black ash on the outside is swept aside, revealing a dramatically darker piece of wood below.

3. Ebonizing: This process makes use of house ingredients. The solution is made from vinegar, which has had steel wool soaking in it for several weeks. When applied to an item, it reacts to the timber's tannins to create a dark shade.

I am not a professional on these darkening approaches, and I would certainly assume they each work better on particular woods than others.

Each approach also has its associated risks, so be sure to do your research study right into each technique to guarantee you know precisely how to do it safely and even properly before attempting.

Durability
Some of the qualities of durable wood are hardness/density, rot resistance and insect resistance.

One point to note is that timber's firmness doesn't have anything to do with the category of " wood."

That classification comes from the seeds of the tree, so do not think that all wood is hard or heavy.

One of the softest timbers is balsa wood, which is classified as a hardwood.

Since we have that cleared up, it allows us to have a look at the characteristics.

Hardness/Density

To provide you with a standard, here are some common timbers you could hear of being utilized often:
Pecan:
Solidity - 1820 lb-ft.
Thickness - 46 lb/ft.

Maple:
Solidity - 1450 lb-ft.
Thickness - 44 lb/ft.

White Oak:
Solidity - 1350 lb-ft.
Density - 47 lb/ft.

White Ash:
Solidity - 1320 lb-ft.
Thickness - 42 lb/ft.

Making use of a denser timber will provide more weight to your piece, which can give it a feel of higher quality.

Making use of a harder timber will give your piece a little additional resistance to damages and also dings, which might be helpful if the part is useful as opposed to decorative.

Rot Resistance/Insect Resistance

Some timber does better with wetness and is also more insect resistant than others, hence making them preferable for outdoor and aquatic applications.

While a lot of protection can be gotten with different finishing techniques, having a wood that is a lot more naturally suited to these scenarios is never a poor thing.

Regarding these two standards, you will simply need to do a little study for every timber you are considering. This can be a great aid in choosing the right wood for a specific project to guarantee it will last a long time.

Workability

The tough or hardwood is more difficult to turn.

Here are the results of the few turnings as per our experience:

The softwoods were simpler to turn and did not blunt the devices as swiftly.

Nevertheless, even a little slip of the tool would certainly put a deep gouge in the timber.

Also, the final projects mar much more easily due to their softness.

Last but not least, you cannot turn these timbers to as tiny size as the hardwoods since they are weaker.

Few more tips

1. Raid scrap bins and also estate sales to gather a range of timbers to try and also see what you like to work with, and what you think looks good.

2. Get a notebook, and each time you turn something, list
   - What kind of timber it was and what you thought about it
   - How it turned.
   - Any type of problems like damaging or tear-out.
   - What kind of finish you used
   - Did you like it on this certain wood?

3. You can also maintain a spreadsheet containing timber species with specifications to ensure that whenever you have a task in mind, you can go to that spreadsheet, see what data is available, filter by specific standards, and hopefully select an excellent timber for the job.

3. Finishing

Sanding Tips

A well-sanded surface is a pre-requisite for high-quality finishing. Below are a few tips for sanding:

- Use high-quality sandpaper, and throw it away when it becomes dull.

- Supply raked/side lighting on the sanding surface area to get any issues.

- Sand your task through all the grits up to 320 or 400 grit without missing any.

- When you believe you are done with sanding, sand one more time with the grain (and the lathe off) to get rid of scratches across the grain.

- Please make sure you don't create heat when sanding, or you'll burnish the surface, making it hard for a finish to adhere to or penetrate.

- Clean the surface with a paper towel before applying the finish.

Power Sander

Finishing Options

There is no single finish suitable for all of your woodturning tasks.

So, where do you start when choosing the appropriate finishing for your project?

The criteria for choosing the ideal finishing for your turning project depends on many factors like:

- Kind of wood
- The project's size and planned use
- Sturdiness
- Drying time
- Required shine (satin or gloss)
- Ease of application
- Solvent or water-based
- Cleanup
- Repairability

Commonly, the novice will find it challenging to achieve a satisfying finish and will certainly use one finish that does it all. However, this is limiting and does not consider how wood needs to consider depending on its final usage.

Is the piece purely ornamental? Are you not sure what you intend to do with the item, or do you want to reveal the beauty of the wood grain?

When viewing a turning project, it is usually the kind of finish or requirement of finish that allows the piece down.

The most significant mistake made by many is to apply too much finish and wind up with streaked or irregular finishes and improperly performed sanding. Here we aim to address these blunders.

Finishing products

Sealants

This team consists of cellulose, acrylic, and shellac ranges. The group also includes pre-catalyzed melamine lacquer, which is a waterproof sealant. These are utilized to seal the timber before using a finish, but they can be used as a final finish. Sanding sealants are diluted by 50%, making use of a suitable thinning agent to enable application over larger areas while remaining wet across the entire item. It also allows the product to flood across the whole project if needed. If left pure, it is commonly challenging to obtain an even coverage with the product directly from the tin.

Waxes

These come in various kinds, such as soft paste waxes or hard stick varieties, and those that can be colored. These are typically best used over a sealant, yet some brand-new types can be used on bare timber.

Resilient hard-wearing finishes

Lacquers and oils fit into this section thoroughly. Some can permeate the lumber; others develop a surface finish and can be found in gloss, satin or matt sheen. Oil is believed to be one of the most durable finishes, but it is not necessarily the best bet for resisting finger marks and dirt contamination.

Beeswax

Decorative finishes

The kind of finish that will customize or alter the appearance of the timber. In some cases, it may cover the product to where it no longer appears like timber. This complex group includes colored stains and also waxes that are related to bare wood along with chemicals such as bleach.

Food safe

If the piece will have contact with food, then the finish has to be food-safe, which suggests it has to comply with existing federal government requirements (if these apply). Conversely, you might utilize pure beeswax, vegetable/mineral oil or liquid paraffin, all of which are applicable, plus lots of other types of finishes your supplier can provide.

Abrasives

These ought to be treated as an additional cutting tool, and you really do get what you pay for where these are concerned. Top-quality abrasives are not low-cost; they need to be fabric-backed and flexible and must not crack when folded. These are generally made of aluminum oxide and are warmth resistant as well as waterproof to some degree. The qualities I use are 80, 120, 180, 240, 320, 400 grit. I usually begin sanding at 80 grit since my turning tools are sharpened on a dry grinder that is fitted with an 80 grit white aloxite grinding wheel, which generates 80 scratches per inch along the cutting edge. 80 grit abrasive will rapidly remove any type of swellings or bumps from the work surface. When working as an apprentice stonemason brightening granite, I remember that if I missed one grade, I had to begin again - there are no short cuts to an excellent finish.

Polishing cloths/papers

Some say clothes, some claim papers, yet I utilize both depending upon the task in hand. Mutton cloth is used for sanding sealer as well as polishing waxes, whereas paper is used for rubbing polish and oils. However, keep in mind that all paper towels have a rough top quality of their own, so it may take time to discover the right one for you. Beginning with a high-quality kitchen paper towel, but ensure you NEVER twist any kind of sprucing up cloth or paper around your fingers. Also, never allow loose ends to track around turning equipment or job.

Wire wool and also Nyweb/Webrax

0000 wire wool is used to reduce finishes as well as sealants. Nyweb and Webrax are synthetic forms of wire wool that do not deteriorate as quickly as the usual wire wool, and they do not leave debris behind as they are made use of. The basic method for finishing is to sand, seal, and then use the finishing coat. Nevertheless, when you are using oil, there is some change in this technique.

Sanding the outside

1. Reduce the lathe speed by half and make use of a piece of abrasive folded in two to sand the outside of your bowl. Keep in mind to maintain the rough moving, never allow it to stop in one area, or scrap it in your last finish coat. Finish the job gradually with the grit from 80-400.

2. With the lathe stationary, use a 25mm (1in) paintbrush and a generous layer of sanding sealer to the dish exterior, moving swiftly to cover the entire surface while it is all damp. Do this quickly, or one-part will dry before an additional coat causing a patchy finish.

3. With the lathe still switched off, get rid of the excess with mutton fabric. When it is dry, turn on the lathe and burnish with the cloth.

4. Making use of Nyweb to cut down the surface area to get rid of the increased grain and excess product. Repeat the process over several layers.

5. Add a moderate layer of paste wax and also allow it to dry completely. Be patient as drying times vary throughout the year.

6. Switch on the lathe and with a clean towel burnish and polish the surface area of the bowl. Move to a clean spot on the cloth first.

Finally, sand the inside

1. Use the same technique to sand the interior of your bowls, but this time around, sand the bowl in the bottom left quarter between the 6 and 9 o'clock placements.

2. Additionally, power sand the interior. Notice the angle at which the head is presented to allow just the lower edge to touch the rotating bowl

3. Attempt a larger sanding pad than you would typically make use of; the larger the pad, the more surface area contact you have - which is better suited to the distance. This larger surface area contact has the advantage of having the ability to level any surface undulations better than a smaller pad.

4. You might additionally utilize an inertia/ passive shear sander to get rid of any radial sanding marks that may still show up externally.

Approach for applying a fueled oil finishing coat

Applying oil takes time; however, it does offer the timber a much deeper sheen as well as richness. When sanding with oil, the amount of fine dust generated in the workshop is much less; it will also fill grain, leaving the wood with a much softer and warmer feel. This is optimal when making things that come into contact with food. Sand as you would typically, making sure no damage is left on the outside of the dish. When completed with oil, it is a great suggestion to cover the lathe bed. Here, I decided to use Danish oil.

1. Place a liberal layer of oil on your bowl, using a 25mm (1in) paintbrush, and leave to sit and trickle for 10 mins. During this time, the oil will soak into the surface of the wood.

2. Replenish the oil and turn on the lathe to its slowest setting. Using old 400 grit abrasive, proceed to abrade the bowl as the fining sand progresses. If it seems too thick and is not spreading properly, add a little bit more oil and continue.

3. Continue to sand the dish until there is a slurry appearing externally on the wood.

4. Wipe clean and completely dry, then run the lathe and burnish with paper. Now set the item to one side in a dust-free area and permit to dry for 24 hours. The next day includes one more layer of oil by brushing on and leaving it to sit for a while, then clean completely dry. Continue until you get the desired finish (I find that two or three coats usually are enough). Once the oil is completely dry, the bowl may well require an extra polish with a reducing substance such as wax. This often suffices to bring the piece to a perfect shine.

Friction polish

This product is usually misused by novices and must only be used on small products, such as light/cord draws and container stoppers. Most manufacturers specify that no sealant is required; however, I find this is not the case - you can achieve a much superior finishing coat when a sealant is used.

1. Sand the item as usual. Fining sand on top allows you to see what you are doing

2. Utilize a small brush to use your chosen fining sand sealer and place a little piece of mutton fabric to the rear of the item with the lathe running - this will certainly catch the excess and burnish it all at once.

3. Continue to burnish. If you have too much product on the item, much of it will be removed during this procedure.

4. Using Nyweb to cut down the surface and remove any further deposit.

5. With your brush dipped into your friction polish, apply as you did the sealant. However, this time utilize a paper towel folded in half.

6. Give the item a final polish using a clean part of the paper.

4. Safety and Best Practices

Safety Instructions

The best advice/quote on woodturning safety I came across is, **"Over-Confidence Is a Woodturners Worst Nightmare."** I couldn't agree more and emphasize the importance of remaining careful at all times while working. Below are the instructions:

Sample accident account 1:

"This is why you use face security. A 25 lb piece of almond just blew up and came off my lathe. My Air Tend Pro is in numerous pieces. I took the hit, yet came out with a couple of small cuts as well as a huge bump on the head. Have to admit I am frightened. The Air Trend is broken, but without it, I would have been. I will certainly boost my safety measures before resuming".

General Instructions

- Please read, understand, and follow all guidelines and safety warnings that include operating your lathe and various other devices before attempting to use them. Failing to comply with safety precautions in your devices' owner's handbooks can lead to severe injury.

- Maintain your lathe as touted in the owner's handbook. Look for damage, bad alignment, binding, and anything that might lead to trouble when you turn the lathe on.

- Do not try to run a lathe without proper training or developing a proper understanding of how it works safely.

- Never operate a lathe or any other power device if you are ill, tired, distracted, or drunk.

- Avoid unanticipated distractions. Keep children and pets away from the lathe area while you're working. Also, see to it that anyone entering the area understands not to distract your focus while the lathe is running.

- Exposure to wood dust can lead to sensitization of the skin and respiratory system, potentially resulting in severe allergic reactions after repeated or direct exposure to lower concentrations of the dust.

- Always operate in a location with appropriate airflow and wear a dust mask, respirator, or air-circulating helmet to prevent hazardous breathing dust. A respirator is an especially excellent concept when sanding and also when working with exotic timbers.

- Keep the flooring in your workspace tidy and uncluttered to prevent slipping or stumbling when you turn.

- See to it, there is sufficient light and also room to move freely.

- Wear a quality compliant face guard while woodturning. Regular spectacles do not provide appropriate security.

- Wear an appropriate hearing defense, specifically while turning.

- Please do not wear anything that might get caught in the lathe while it is running. That means no rings, watches, or other jewelry.

- Wear tops with short sleeves, or roll up long sleeves. Do not put on loose garments. Tie long hair back. Do not wear gloves while turning.

Using Turning Tools Safely

Use the tools just as they are made after reading the user manual and guidelines. Unexpected use might lead to severe injury or death. For example, you cannot use a Spindle Roughing Gouge on a bowl. Spindle roughing gouges are not built to manage the stress associated with face turning and could break, possibly causing significant injury.

Working on Lathe

- Position yourself on the appropriate side of the lathe; the timber should rotate towards you.

- Inspect the lathe speed setup before starting the lathe.

- Begin the slowly and keep it there up until the workpiece is transformed, round and balanced.

- Maintain a slow-moving rate for larger-diameter turnings. Suit the speed to the transforming project.

- Always shut off the lathe and allow it to come to a complete stop before changing the placement of the tool rest or tool rest holder (banjo). Never change the tool rest while the lathe is running. Never stop a rotating work surface with your hand.

- Before starting the lathe, see to it that the workpiece is mounted safely between the drive center of the headstock and the tailstock or held firmly with a four-jaw chuck. When the workpiece is protected in a chuck, use the tailstock whenever feasible as an added step of safety.

- Set the tool rest as close to the workpiece as you can, but make sure that it won't get caught in any part of the workpiece during turning. Rearrange the tool rest after removing excess timber from your project work surface to maintain needed support for your tools.

- Before starting the lathe, always rotate the workpiece by hand to see if it clears the bed of the lathe, the tool rest, and the tool rest owner (also called the banjo). Always check to see that all nuts and bolts are locked tight.

- Make sure that all guards, belt covers, and various other security attributes are correctly installed and are secure before starting the lathe. Eliminate any loosened products, tools, or unnecessary workpieces from the workspace before starting the lathe.

- Check your work surface for any divides, splits, inclusions, or various other issues that can compromise the stability of the wood and perhaps cause the work surface to come apart or come off the lathe. Do not try to turn pieces that have substantial problems.

- Continue to inspect the work surface as you turn, stopping the lathe regularly to examine for problems exposed by the elimination of the product.

- Never leave the lathe running on its own.

- Keep the turning tools sharp, which will leave a better surface and need much less pressure to cut the wood, reducing the likelihood of an injury. Never force a dull tool.

- Preserve a balanced position. Do not overreach or utilize extreme pressure to do any machine operation.

- Always keep fingers behind the tool rest when turning. Severe injury can result if your fingers get captured in between the tool rest and the turning stock.

- Use both hands to keep complete control of your turning devices, with one hand forward to regulate the cutting side and the other back.

- To decrease the likelihood of hazardous catches, always bring the tool to the device rest initially, see to it you've got it secured there, and use it to change the spinning work surface.

- Always relocate the banjo out of the way and get rid of the tool rest before fine sanding a workpiece on the lathe. If you do not, you risk obstructing your fingers or twisting your wrist.

- Never utilize a cloth to apply surface or polish while a job is rotating on the lathe. The cloth might be captured and pull your hand right into the turning, possibly causing severe injury.

Sample accident account 2 :

I was just reminded again of the relevance of wearing safety tools. The bowl I was turning came apart at one of the development rings. There were no signs when I inspected earlier.

Workspace setting

The location, particularly around your wood lathe, should be clear and without debris, devices, or any barriers. Power cords present a risk when they are straight underfoot. I keep my power cords behind the lathe, where I will not get tangled in them.

Wood shavings begin to build up and can become a threat. My woodturning coach has an ideology that a thin layer of shavings on the ground is a good thing. I have also dropped many small items like screws and hex wrenches to have them roll away completely. I have used a handheld magnetic strip on a deal to run over the shavings and relocate much of those dropped objects.

Likewise, I have a comfortable, supported anti-fatigue floor covering on the flooring where I stand while turning bowls, making my lathe turning time very comfortable. At a minimum, the anti-fatigue mat prevents my legs from feeling sore after a full day of turning. And the mat is very easy to lift as I whisk dust away from my workplace.

Wearing Safety Gear

Whenever around a lathe, it's a great habit to use safety gear. The essential woodturning safety devices are safety glasses, full face shields, safety shoes, respirators, and an efficient air filtering system.

Sample Workspace

Safety Gear

Lighting

Make sure to have a lot of good light at the lathe. A flexible light or 2 is essential to light up the straight work area. An excellent movable light, angled from the side, helps to clear up high and low places on a dish surface area. Use a flexible light such as this to brighten your lathe completely.

Woodturners physical and mental state

The state of your physical and mental being is as crucial or even more vital than whatever mechanical work you are doing.

 If you aren't feeling good, are tired out or intoxicated, it's best to turn off the lathe until the next day.

Give yourself a break and don't push if your physical state might impair your judgment and motor abilities.

It can be challenging to self detect problems, as we are generally the last to admit we ought to stop. Small errors such as catches that don't usually happen can be an early sign that it is time for a break.

A woodworker working on a lathe

Working on a Lathe: best practices

Before we can begin to turn, we need to make sure the location around the lathe is well-defined and prepared.

Any added tools and products need to be well away from the maker.

Several lathes have a tool tray for chuck keys, hex wrenches, as well as other accessories underneath the bed. This is fine to utilize, and any un-needed tools can sit in the provided place, and they will not rapidly come loose.

A sample lathe

Before fixing wood bowl blank to the lathe, relocate the tool rest, banjo, and tailstock, so they are entirely out of the way and make sure the power is shut off, and set the lathe speed to the most appropriate for your project.

Faceplate setting

If you choose to mount the bowl blank to a faceplate, make use of top quality timber screws and not drywall screws.

Drywall screws are much thinner and also made more cheaply compared to timber screws, and they can snap off under the high torque while transforming.

Also, make sure the screws are long enough to securely hold the bowl on place, but not so long as to hinder your desired dish shape. When your bowl space has been prepared and all set, it's time to bring it to the lathe. With the power off, rotate the dish blank by hand and watch to see if it settles away quickly.
 If this does happen, it may imply the bowl is off-center.

Faceplate mounted on wood piece

Standing clear, turn the lathe on and gradually accelerate the speed. If there is a remarkable vibration at slow-moving rates, reconsider focusing the faceplate or chuck.

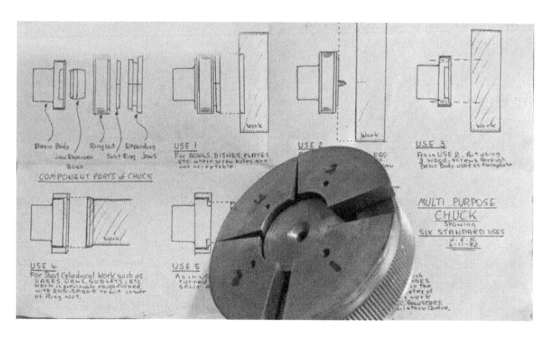

A multipurpose chuck

If the piece you're working with is off-center on purpose, understand that you will certainly have to turn the bowl at a much slower rate as a result of this inequality.

Lathe optimum speed

For checking the lathe's optimum balance speed, the general rule is to slowly boost the lathe rate until the wood piece starts to vibrate, then start decreasing the speed up until it stops shaking. That point is the optimum speed required for turning efficiently.

Check contact with a lathe.

Once the blank is placed and ready, bring the banjo and tool rest into location. With the lathe off, turn the headstock hand handles and rotate the item extensively several times to make sure no part of the dish blank will contact the tool rest, banjo, or any other part of the lathe.

Woodturner's position

Each cut made while turning a timber bowl requires to be thought out a little bit in advance. Here is an excellent method to start with when you first begin, that will progress into a habit.

I usually start by turning and forming an all-time low of the bowl from the tailstock side. While I'm doing these cuts, I do not stand in front of the lathe in the path of turning. I have had tenons stop working, sending out bowls to the flooring and bark flying off.

From the tailstock side, I usually have an excellent position to watch the action as a viewer without being in touch with any of the follies.

Even while making a leveling cut across the bottom of the turning bowl space, place most of the body to the left, or headstock side if you are right-handed, so just the arms and hands are in front of the rotating item.

Mobile Lathe

In case of a mobile lathe, move it sideways or at a place where you will find woodturning easy.

While turning to the tailstock side, bring it with you if you move to the headstock side. It requires to be in a location that can be accessed without crossing the path of the woodturning wood piece.

In case the lathe does not have this feature, and the switch is only accessible if you reach over the wood, consider stepping back from the lathe and making a broader course to the switch if something goes wrong.

Tool Rest

A tool rest is an adjustable horizontal bar for supporting a hand tool when turning.

The tool rest needs to be as close to the turning blank as the tool needs.

Sample Toolrest

Every tool is different, and the tool rest must be adjusted for each one.

Lathe speed

There is no perfect speed for turning a wood bowl. Yet there are some things of which to be mindful of when adjusting the speed. As a whole, I don't turn bowls any faster than 1000 r.p.m. There is hardly ever a need for speeds much quicker than this.

Sample Accident 3:

My first lathe had a rotating head so you could work straight in front of you, and I used it that way almost exclusively. This required an extension arm between the banjo and tool-rest that brought the tool-rest above the center of rotation.

I did not realize how dangerous that was. I broke two banjos, a Sorby gouge, and smashed the crap out of one of my favorite fingers more than once.

Stop and change the tool rest

Before moving and changing the tool rest, stop the lathe. It takes a little bit more time; however, it's far better than getting slapped by a rotating bowl on the lathe.

Keep changing the tool rest, so it is positioned to offer you the upper hand leverage, literally, as well as produce the very best cut from the tool you're using.

Finishing

When you're sanding, or whenever there are dust fragments in the air, make sure to put on a dust mask or respirator. If you are determined to turn the lathe while sanding, do so at a slow rate.

Before begin, move the tool rest, banjo, and tailstock far from the turning bowl, so they don't present a pinch point.

This is a big deal, and also I see people doing this regularly. Never use any fabric textiles to apply a finish to a **rotating bowl**. You may utilize a towel to use finishes such as oils if the lathe is off.

Instead, utilize paper towels to apply to finish products to a rotating bowl. If the paper towel gets caught, it will just rip away and create no damage.

Post Turning

Cleaning up the lathe location and put away all the tools, devices, and materials, especially the finishing materials. Dispose of used paper towels and cloths according to the manufacturer's referrals on the item packaging. Tidy up all those shavings and prepare the area for the next time it will be utilized.

4. Ten Beginner Woodturning Projects

1. Bowl

Step 1: First, a little information regarding the tools required for woodturning. Here are the devices I used on this project. There are much cheaper variations of all of these things if you are on a budget. Below is a sample of tools used for the project:

- Chuck.
- Cole Jaw Set.
- Laguna 1412, Bandsaw
- Easy Timber Devices Carbide Turning Devices.
- Lathe.

Step 2: Cut the wood

Cut your log in half lengthwise; after that, cut a square item for one of the bisections.

Mark the wood as well as place your faceplate.

Make sure to use strong screws here; drywall screws do not have a great deal of sheer toughness.

Step 3: Roughing out

To begin, rough out the bottom of your bowl.

You want to bring the outside right into shape and then start to develop the form of your bowl.

Get rid of as little material as you can, or else, you'll end up with a smaller bowl than required.

When the bottom is ready, cut a tenon and place the bowl right into your chuck jaws. Again, this may be an aftermarket product, depending on your lathe.

With the bowl on the chuck, start to rough out from within your bowl.

You want the outside as well as inside walls of your bowl to be parallel. Wall surface thickness is an individual choice.

Ensure you look for cracks in the process; logs are full of them. If you have a huge one, you can stabilize it with epoxy.

Step 4: Sand the bowl from inside

After getting the desired shape in the previous step, increase the speed of the lathe, and take shallow passes. This will result in a beautiful, smoother surface, given the tools are appropriately sharp.

Post that applies to sand to the inside surface of the bowl while it is still mounted on the lathe. You can use sandpaper from 120 to 600 grit.

Step 5: Smooth the base of the bowl

Next off, place your bowl into a collection of Cole jaws on your chuck. There are various other methods to do this; however, Cole's jaws are quite fantastic for this kind of task.

Cutaway the tenon you created in the previous step and afterward began to make the bottom of the bowl smoother.

If the bottom is concave, the bowl will rest flat. It is essential to complete the sanding procedure once more. You could start at 80 grit in case of some more tear-out.

Step 6: Finishing

The next step is to spray polyurethane for the finish. It is simple and quick. You can also apply colors if you wish.

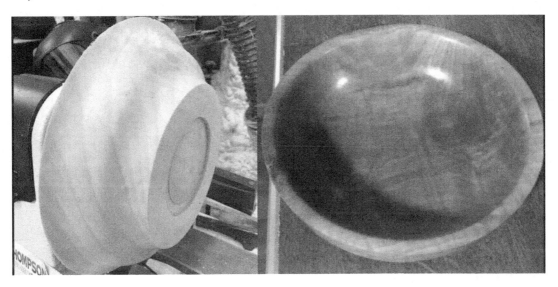

2. Rolling Pin

Tools Required

- Spindle gouge

- Roughing gouge

- Round nosed scarper

- Sycamore wood

- Parting Tool

- Lathe

- Take a wood plank with the dimensions as per your requirement; let's say here we take 16 inches by 3. Make sure that the tool rest is square to the bed. Ensure that everything is locked down properly before starting the lathe.

- Start with a roughing gouge. Repeat the same step at the other end to make it cylindrical.

- Now mark the handles on the cylinder on both sides. Here we take half inches from both sides and mark them as the end of the handles.

- After that, mark the handle length on both sides, as shown above.

- Use the parting tool on the half-inch marks on both sides, as shown below. (the line at the end on both sides)

- For making handles, first, use a roughing gouge and then spindle gouge, as shown in the pictures below.

- Now use a spindle gouge to make the handle of the desired same radius as the end of the handle.

- Apply sanding paper starting from 150 grit to 180 grit. Wear a respirator here and keep the paper moving all the time.

- Finish it off by applying food-safe oil rub it along the grain. Put 2-3 layers of coating.

3. Baseball Bat

Tools Required:

- 36" wood bat blank

- Wood lathe

- Turning devices

- Square

- Outside calipers

- Sandpaper

- Oil/varnish finish

- High-quality Japanese saw

Picking the wood:

Start with finding a blank of either maple or north ash. The size should be approximately 3" round and 36" long.

The straighter and tighter the grain, the much less chance it will break when you use it.

Material that's been graded for making bats is far better than what you discover at the neighborhood hardwood shop.

You can find some great sources online.

If you cannot discover a round blank, you can start with a blank that's square in cross-section.

Then chamfer the long edges to make it octagonal in cross-section.

The blank needs to be 3" longer than the final length to allow for waste at both ends.

Noting the center

The following action is to mark the center of the cylindrical tube on both sides.

You can make use of a center finder if you have one.

Otherwise, a good technique is to use a square to etch a perfect angle inside the circle.

Draw the line where the legs of the square intersect the circumference. That line will be the center.

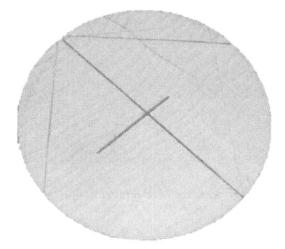

Repeat the same thing once again after revolving the square 90 degrees, as well as the intersection of those two lines is the center.

At the center, use an awl to make a hole that the centers will certainly fit into.

Roughing the blank

Mount the blank on the lathe.

I use a live facility at the tailstock and a step facility at the headstock.

I mount the bat so that the barrel will be closest to the headstock.

I locate it more comfortable to turn in this manner, and it seems to vibrate less; however, if you mount it with the barrel at the tailstock, the majority of the cuts are "downhill."

Turn the blank right into a cylindrical tube, ensuring it goes at the very least to 2.75" along with its size.

Adjust the speed to 800 rpm as it is an excellent rate.

Marking the bat

We can mark out the bat by laying pencil lines every 3" on the blank, including the end of the handle and the barrel.

Hold a pencil approximately across the spinning space as well as it will leave a clear line.

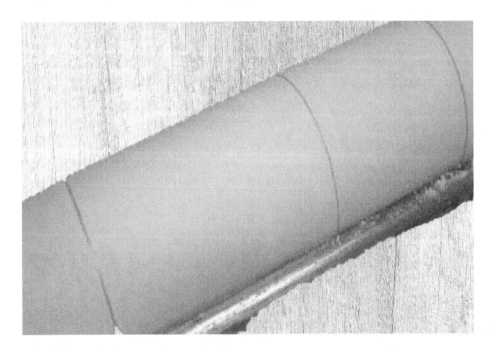

Gauging the deepness

We use a parting tool to make a small channel at the end of the barrel.

The diameter of this cut should be left at about 1/8" larger than the finished dimension.

Starting from the barrel down, cut to depth the first 3 or 4 of these marks

You can add about 1/16" to the measurement for cutting and sanding. Using a parting chisel, cut the blank until the caliper barely slips through.

Forming/shaping the barrel

The roughing gouge can be used again to eliminate a lot of the waste between the cuts.

Next, turn the lathe up to 1200-1600 rpm.

I try to keep a fair contour between the cuts by focusing on the rear of the barrel's silhouette.

I then use a skew cut to smooth the surface area.

While I'm pointing out the tools I make use of, other transforming devices can work just as well.

I usually sand the barrel with 100 grit sandpaper (or whatever the surface coating requires) before I go on to cut the remainder of the bat.

This enables me to get a great of surface area sanded before the bat becomes too whippy on the lathe.

Making the handle and knob

Continue utilizing the parting tool to note the suitable depth of the cuts.

Utilize the spindle gouge, or the skew sculpt to level the curve in between the networks cut with the parting gouge.

The shapes and sizes of handles vary greatly and are a matter of personal choice-- they don't impact the efficiency.

Sanding

Depending on the surface quality and level of the contour, you'll need different amounts of sanding.

If the surface area is rough and the profile not perfectly smooth, you need to begin with 80 grit sandpaper.

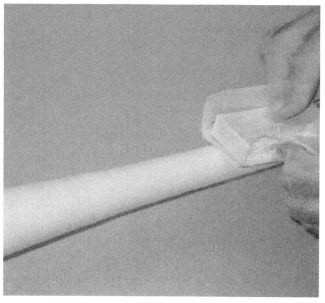

To help smooth the form and also not make the flaws even worse, it's useful to place a small block of wood inside the sandpaper, so you're not merely brightening the tops and also valleys.

If the surface area is smoother, you can start sanding with 100 or 120 grit sandpaper.

I generally sand in numerous steps up to 220 but have been cured of trying to sand it smoother by viewing how my kids throw the bats around and cover them with yearning tar.

Finishing:

A blend of oil and varnish seems to be the best finish. You can acquire these sorts of coatings in the equipment shop or make your very own combination.

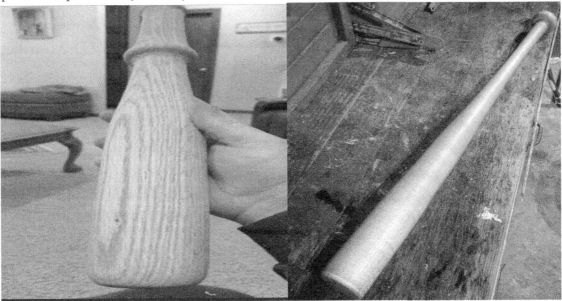

You can place a couple of coats of finish on while the bat is still mounted on the lathe.

I load a dust cloth up with the combination and hold it up to the rotating bat.

Trimming the ends

Use the skew chisel held vertically to make very clean cuts on the end grain.

If you're making use of a gouge or a scarping tool, take care here because tidying up the marks left in the long run grain is most difficult.

After that, get rid of some excess with a parting chisel and also leave a shoulder for the saw to ride on.

Cut the projection on top of the barrel to about an inch across.

After that, remove the bat from the lathe, use small Japanese saw to cut off the little nubs, and then sand the ends.

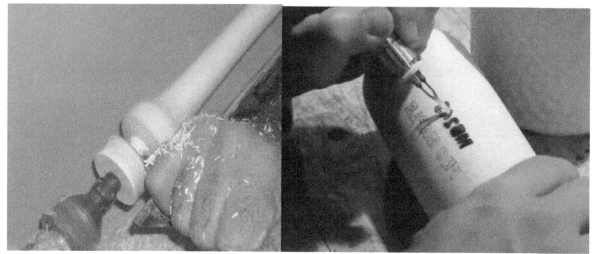

The last action is to use even more coating. I usually wet sand the surface now with 400 grit sandpaper as well as do as numerous layers as my persistence or children allow before one of them wants to take it out and hit with it.

4. Wood Canteen

Tools Required

- A robust lathe with a faceplate

- A big drill bit (around 1") and also a way to transform it

- A transforming cut carve

- A straight transforming chisel

- Sandpaper

- A saw

- Wood

- Glue

- Wood coating

Drill and Set the Center

The first step is the standard woodturning procedure.

Drill the mouth of the bottle initially and utilize it to establish the centers.

This will certainly ensure you are starting with a concentric form with the mouth in the precise center.

For example, you can use a scrap of 6" x6" Douglas fir.

The very first turning has to be finished up smoothly at this step.

Sand and do whatever else to complete this surface area, you will certainly not be remounting it again.

Removing the Shanks
The piece must then be remounted to bowl-out the interior from one side.

You can use a bandsaw to cut off items from two sides, giving a flat mounting surface for the faceplate.

Conserve those two shanks of timber; you will be making use of at least one of them to top the large opening you will now bore in the side of the container.

Bowling-out the Inside

This action is the same as bowl-turning, other than you will be turning an asymmetrical item. If your lathe has rate control, ease into it.

You can safely rough-cut a piece such as this at 700rpm.

Your chisel will wish to stray from the center, so make your cuts carefully and perpendicular to the surface you're cutting into.

Start from the boundary and move in towards the center, resisting the outward force.

If you drilled the mouth sufficiently deep, you need to break through to it.

When dealing with complicated wood, you can leave a lot of thinner walls.

If you have the skill and also a proper square carve, make an action on the edge of the dish to far better seat the cap in the future.

Make it Attractive

This next action is much more decorative than anything else, though it will include some balance to the piece, and all noticeable surface areas will have been turned.

The jug must be turned around so you can function on the opposite side. You can screw the faceplate to the containers inside the wall surface; however, only if the screws do not strike your chisel as it digs into the item.

Turning the Cap

Remember those shanks you removed in Step 2?

You will be using one, preferably the one from the side that was hollowed.

Glue it to a block of timber and install it on the faceplate.

Turn it sufficient to make it perfectly round and provide it a lip to better seat inside the jug's hollowed bowl.

Use calipers to get the right measurements.

If you have threading devices, this would be an excellent opportunity to use them, though threads might make it challenging to get the grain direction to match. Cut the cap off the block.

The sawn surface does not need to look great since it will get on the jug within the jug. It merely offers it a quick sanding.

Finishing

If you wish to make this a functional canteen, utilize a food-safe coating like pure tung oil on the inside and outside.

There are other safe finishes available, though they do not have the durability and damp resistance you would certainly want for the inside of a liquid vessel.

5. Candle Holder

Tools Required:

- Maple wood

- Waste woodblock

- Lathe

- Glue

- Roughing gouge

- Wax and Mineral Oil

- Sandpaper

Steps

- Glue the piece of maple on the waste block, as shown below. Leave it for few minutes and then start the turning process.

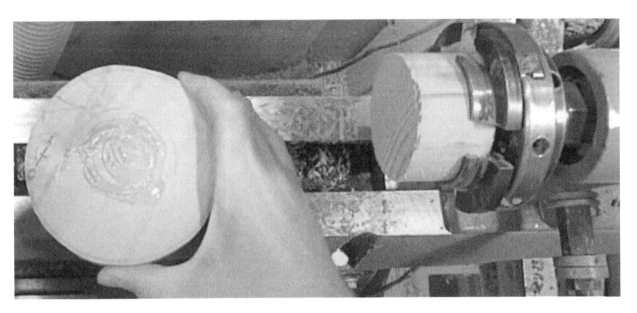

- Measure the radius of the candle on the back of the maple wood piece to make a fitting hole on it.

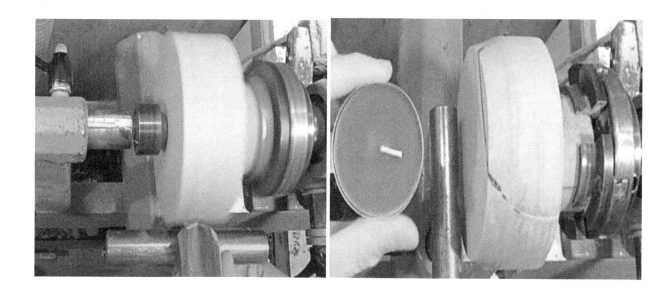

- Now give a slant shape to the wood piece using scraper and gouge as shown below till the shape becomes like the picture shown below.

- The next step is sanding and then put on finishing wax and mineral oil.

- Remove the wood piece and see the candle slot. Then put it back on the lathe to work on the bottom side of the candle holder. Apply sanding and finishing to this surface also done earlier.

- Put the candle in the slot and cherish your work!

6. Spoon

Tools Required:

- Maple wood

- Waste woodblock

- Lathe

- Roughing gouge

- Wax and Mineral Oil

- Sandpaper

Steps

- Take a piece of the maple with these dimensions: Length: 6 & 1/2 inches, Breadth: 1 & 1/2 inches, Height: 3/4 inch

- Mark the handle of the spoon with a pencil, as shown.

- Use a band saw to cut along the marked lines.

- Mark the centers on both ends, as shown below.

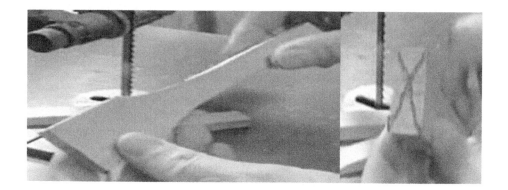

- Put the wood piece in the chuck and start turning.

- Use a spindle gouge to make a concave surface for the spoon head.

- Start on the lathe and use the roughing gouge.

- Turn the wood till you get the desired handle shape.

- Do the sanding using regular sanding paper with grit, depending on the roughness of the wood.

- Use a carving chisel to further shape up the scoop of the spoon.

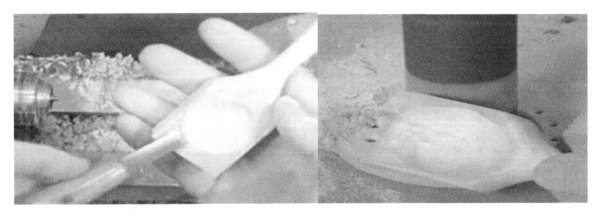

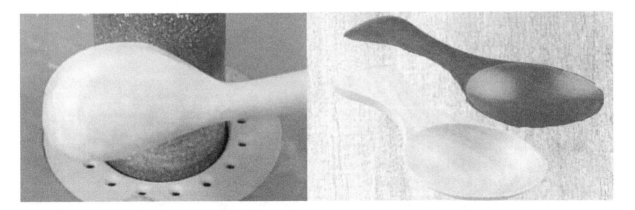

- Lastly, apply food-safe finishing wax and mineral oil of your choice.

7. Ladle

Tools Required:

- Woodblock for scoop and handle

- Lathe

- Roughing gouge

- Wax and Mineral Oil

- Driller

- Sandpaper

Steps

- Take a cubical woodblock for making scoop of the ladle. Draw a circle on the face with a pencil and cut as much as possible before putting on the lathe.

- Run the lathe and use a roughing gouge to shape up the scoop, as shown in the below pictures.

- As the overall shape becomes oval, start with making a concave surface for the scoop, as shown below.

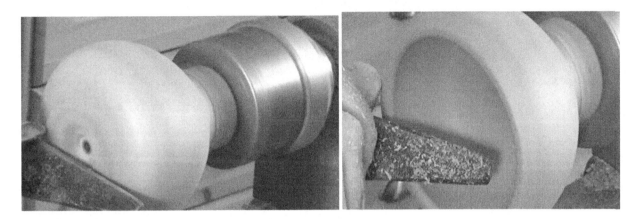

- Next, move on to make the handle. Put the piece of wood on the lathe and start turning.

- Make a hole in the scoop to fit in the handle. Use glue additionally to strengthen the bond further.

- Apply sanding in both the wood pieces.

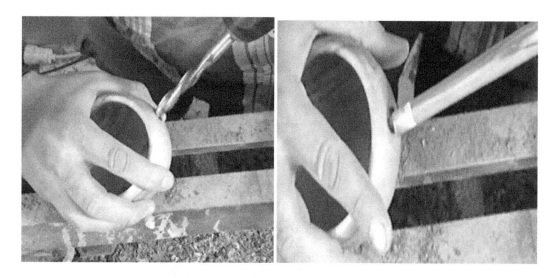

- Apply food-safe wax and mineral oil of your choice.

8. Wooden Ring

Tools Required:

- Steel Ring

- Wood plank

- Waste block

- Lathe

- Roughing gouge

- Finishing coating (CA)

- Driller

- Sandpaper

- Rake scraper

- Putty knife

- Glue

- Double-sided tape

- Derlin ring

Steps

- Take a steel ring upon which you would like to have a wooden cover to make a comfort ring.

- Select a suitable plank. It's a critical step. The plank should be a little wider than the ring, completely dried and stabilized. It should not crack up upon working.

- Lay some 120 grit sandpaper on a flat surface and sand one side flat. Once it's flat, apply double-sided tape to the reference face, as shown below.

- Now start turning the wood but mounting it on a waste block using double-sided tape.

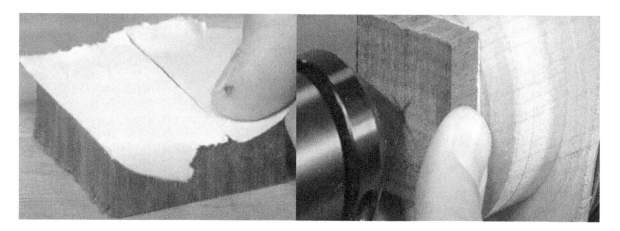

- Peel off the tape backing and line up the center mark with a revolving Center, and with the tailstock in place, rough turn the blank to round.

- Select a drill bit that is approximately half the diameter of the ring core to make a pilot hole. Mount the bit in a drill chuck and drill entirely through the blank, as shown above.

- Using a narrow scraper or skew, laid flat on its side, open up the drilled hole until the ring core fits snugly. Keep testing the ring fitment till it goes inside the wooden hole. Keep 3-4 rings of different sizes as your one ring becomes loosely fitted, you can try the other ones.

- Work on the side of the blank and turn it down until it's just a hair wider than the ring core. Try not to scratch the ring core with the tool. Now carefully peel the blank off the waste block using a putty knife.

- Next, sand the steel ring and glue it up inside the wooden ring. (may use epoxy or CA glue). After gluing the ring inside, swipe away the extra glue outside.

- After the glue is cured, mount the ring between the Delrin ring bushings on a pen mandrel. Start turning it carefully as its delicate.

- You can use a scraper when turning rings because it's not aggressive and easy to control.

- Once it's turned to shape, sand the blank through 320 grit or higher.

- Next, put up a finishing coat, which is shiny (as it is jewelry). You can put 8-10 coats of CA for a shiny surface.

- Enjoy the ring or gift it to a loved one.

9. Turning Tops

Tools Required:

- Spindle Gouge

- Roughing Gouge

- Nose scraper

- Wood plank

- Parting tool

- Lathe

- Roughing gouge

- Finishing coating

- Sandpaper

Steps

- Take up the wood plank and put it on the lathe, as shown below.

- Apply spindle gouge with your fingers running against the tool rest.

- Choose a wood plank large enough for your chuck.

- Use a parting tool to make a tenon.

- Take a sample turning top and make a line at the place with the maximum width of the tabletop. Draw a second line denoting the bottom of the piece. Use a bevel to shape up the handle further.

- After the handle, work on the lower part of the turning top. You have to make it slanted using the bevel and gouge, as shown below. Now use the sandpaper and make it smoother.

- Use denatured alcohol or methylated spirits to clean up and then use Danish oil. Wait for it to dry and then buff it to shine. You can also use shellac.

- The next step is cutting the top from the rest of the wood. Do not use the parting tool bur spindle gouge instead. Apply sanding and finishing to the bottom tip on the recently cut top.

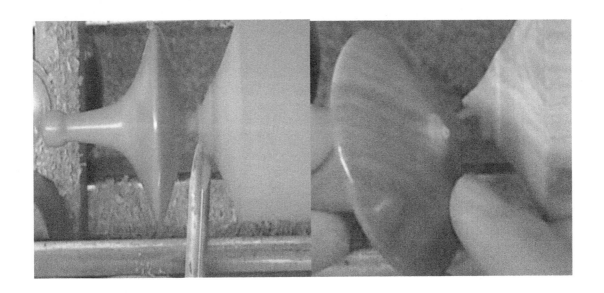

- Now you have your tabletop to play with, enjoy!

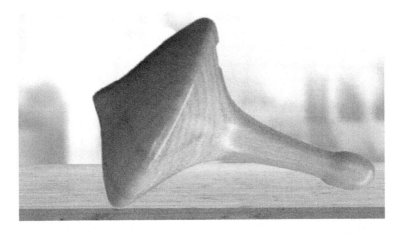

10. Mushroom

Tools Required:

- Spindle Gouge

- Roughing Gouge

- Nose scraper

- Wood plank

- Parting tool

- Lathe

- Roughing gouge

- Finishing coating

- Sandpaper

Steps

- Take a wooden plank and mark centers at the top and bottom face. Now set it into the lathe machine as shown below.

- Use a diamond-tipped parting tool. Now start turning the correct size of tenon as per the set of jaws you have.

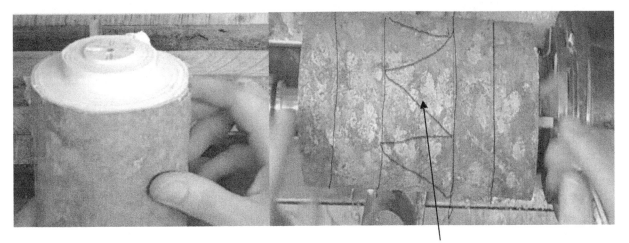

Tenon made as per jaws   Mark the area to be removed

- For rounding off the top, you can use a bowl gouge, spindle gouge, or a skew chisel. The next step is cutting the middle portion, as shown above, as "area to be removed." You can use the bowl gouge again and start eating away at the nub. Now the tailstock may be removed using spindle gouge as shown below.

- Make the center thinner with a realistic bulge at the bottom using spindle gouge. Also, make the roof of the umbrella more natural by undercutting from below (it shouldn't be a flat surface). Also, cut off the base as per the line you have drawn for the base.

- Next, sand it down to 400-600 grit and apply Danish oil as finishing coating.

- The last step is to cut off the base of the mushroom from the waste block:

5. Tips, Glossary, and Conclusion

Points to think of if you wish to take woodturning to the next level and start making money. I am throwing a few pointers you can add as per your thought process

- How is your item/project in comparison to your competition in the area you would like to sell in?

- Can you generate sellable quality regularly?

- How long does it take you to produce your products?

- How much do you charge an hour, is it sustainable?

- What are the expenses, and can they be recovered from selling the products?

- Do you have a process and support system in place to produce multiple products?

- Do you wish to make what you want or what the client desires?

- Do you wish to invest 12 hrs a day in the workshop?

- Do you have plans /means to advertise your product in the target market?

- If you are going down the exhibit or gallery path, what's the standard of the display at the gallery?

This is the kind of pastime where people can pick up skills extremely quickly and produce excellent work, yet to take it to the next level needs a lot of business acumen. Do you wish to transform your hobby into a task that you may or may not like going ahead? You are the best person to decide what you want from the craft.

Woodturning Safety And Security Tips

Woodturning is a sub-niche of woodworking, and experienced woodturners can make every little thing from elaborate pieces of furniture to wood clocks, lamps, kids' toys, as well as fashion jewelry boxes and jewelry.

The layout selections are only limited by the skill and the creative imagination of the woodturner.

For professional woodturners and home hobby enthusiasts, woodturning is a rewarding and relaxing pastime; however, much like any other leisure activity involving power tools and sharp devices, there is the risk of severe and even life-threatening injuries.

Though minor scratches are inevitable, following basic woodturning safety and security suggestions can protect against severe injury.

Outfit for Safety

Flying wood chips can create significant injuries to the eyes and face. Wear security goggles that also give side protection.

When needing to work with loud machinery such as a power saw, wear an ear cover.

Pull long hair back from the face, tie it up, and safeguard it under a cap or scarf so it cannot get entangled in the machinery.

Wear fitting clothes, given that baggy clothing, may get stuck.

No fashion jewelry should be worn, particularly rings, loose-fitting bracelets, or watches. Similarly, never wear a tie while turning.

Bulky tools can fall and damage the feet, so avoid open-toe footwear or shoes and wear safety boots.

Woodturning can send a great deal of dust that can get right up into the lungs and create breathing troubles. Always wear a dust mask when fining sand or turning timber. Some face guards on the market now consist of filters that clean the air efficiently before it is inhaled.

Running the Lathe

Background understanding is essential when you begin turning.

Find a skilled turner and also see the appropriate strategies of running the lathe for different projects.

Check out woodturning publications and instruction video clips, as well as programs.

Thoroughly evaluate user manuals and warnings included with the lathe and all other equipment before using them.

Beginning the lathe at the lowest setting when turning it on, and then get used to the speed needed. As a basic rule of thumb, larger pieces of hardwood require slower speeds, as do unbalanced pieces.

When the lathe has been switched on, it should never be left neglected. If taking a break, turn it off and wait until it comes to a complete stop.

Before trying out a brand-new strategy, practice the move in your mind and then on an item of softwood.

More than normal vibrations, weird smells or noises might indicate that the lathe is not working correctly. Shut off the lathe, and check over the device extensively before returning to use.

Routinely evaluate the problem of the lathe for the right positioning and procedures.

Style of working space

Establish the workspace to produce the optimal environment.

Proper lighting is essential to see clearly while working.

Extension cables can cause electrical shocks and are also a tripping hazard, so it is advisable not to use them.

To give sufficient airflow against dust, it is recommended that a dust removal system be used.

The workshop should also feature windows that can be opened up for airflow and ventilation.

Clean the workspace after each session.

This consists of cleaning all tools and also placing them up out of the reach of youngsters.

Clear the floor and take all equipment off the floor.

Make sure that all the tools are correctly sharpened before starting each project.

Emergency Readiness

Don't panic in case of an accident.

Examine the injury and assess the damage; if the wound needs instant medical attention, call the emergency response number of your location.

Keep a phone in the workshop to obtain fast access to emergency medical services.

To deal with minor cuts and abrasions, maintain an emergency first-aid kit in the workspace.

Always keep a fire extinguisher ready at your workplace and keep it properly maintained.

A running sink in the workstation will be required if dust fragments or chemicals get into the eyes.

In the case of chemical burns, water can likewise be used.

Common Sense Safety Tips

Take notice of your body. Never try to turn if feeling tired out, after drinking, or when heavily medicated.

Keep within the limits of your understanding. Beginners should stay with the processes they understand.

Beginners trying advanced methods by themselves can have alarming repercussions.

Glossary

Woodturning
The craft of using the lathe to generate objects from wood.

Green Timber
Fresh cut logs or timber. They are generally utilized to draft different kinds of projects such as bowls, to permit them to dry completely, and then return to for further work later on. Often used to a final type and enabled to warp creatively. The term refers to damp logs.

Open Form
The lip of the form is continually increasing in diameter in open form vessels.

Closed-Form
In this type of vessel, the lip of the form increases from the bottom decreases eventually towards the top.

Hollow Type
A closed-form with a tiny opening on top.

Pin
A narrow turned piece with the grain ranging from one end to the other.

Lathe
A tool that holds and turns wood while a tool is utilized to shape the wood piece.

Headstock
The part of the lathe that contains the driving mechanism for the lathe.

It is connected to the lathe bed and usually has a spindle for installing faceplates.

Tailstock
An assembly is moving along the bed of the lathe, which can also be secured at any desired placement on the bed.

It consists of a spindle that holds dead centers or live facilities and is typically, however, not solely used in pin switching.

Faceplate

A steel or wood disk installed on the headstock pin and Woodstock is attached to it with screws and holes in the faceplate.

Chuck

Any type of device that holds wood in either jaws or wood is fitted into a cylinder of the chuck.

The chuck is installed on the headstock spindle for working the wood.

Gouge

A device that has a flute and creates a cutting action instead of scraping.

Roughing Gouge

A gouge with fairly thick wall surfaces is used to outline and round stock to a cylindrical shape very quickly.

The edges are not ground back, and the angle around the entire side is about 40 degrees.

By rolling the gouge, you can use the whole side.

Bowl Gouge

A gouge that has a medium to deep flute and is used to rough out and complete the insides of bowls.

Side-Ground Gouge

A gouge that has one or both sides ground back and can be used in a range of placements for harsh, smooth, large scrapes, etc.

Spindle Gouge

A gouge that has a shallow flute and is utilized to generate grains and curves mostly in spindle work (i.e., in between facilities).

Skew Chisel

Given the name since the cutting edge is at an angle to the tool's side.

The cutting side is usually ground to an angle of 70 degrees.

Parting Device

It is used to make slim recesses or grooves to the desired deepness or to part an item from the lathe.

A typical kind would be the diamond shape, with the center being thicker than the outside to offer the device clearance and avoid friction.

Beading Device

Generally constructed of 3/8th inch square supply and also having angles in 30 degrees and 45 degrees and likewise can be utilized as a parting device.

Scraper

Any type of tool that scratches the timber off rather than cutting or shearing the wood.

A scraper will generally have a very blunt angle and a burr on the edge that does the actual scratching of the wood. It can be likened somewhat to a cabinet scraper.

Chucking

Installing or holding a work surface on some piece of equipment aside from faceplate.

Parting tool

We utilize a parting device to reduce a section of wood to a particular size.

Reverse Chucking

The approach of turning around a form on the lathe to avert the waste near the bottom as well as finish off the piece.

Conclusion

Woodturning in all its kinds is an incredibly popular and pleasurable hobby. The acquisition of good quality lathe, other tools along with a collection of books(online and hardcopy) showcasing and explaining the wood turner's skills will make sure many happy and constructive hours off turning.

Also, we have discussed that safety is of the utmost priority while woodturning. No book or online resource is a substitute for live training, but a supplement to it. Therefore always contact an expert in case of any confusion and follow best practices while woodturning.

This brings to a close the current discussion. It would be very much appreciated if you could leave your feedback on the purchasing platform.

Stephen Fleming

Other Books in DIY Series

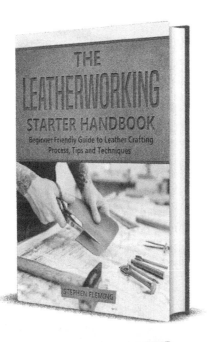

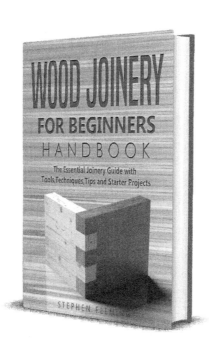

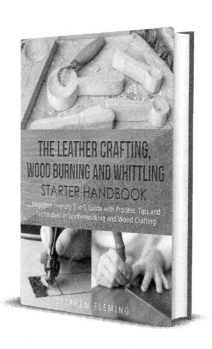

Made in the USA
Monee, IL
07 December 2020